Stop The Killing

Richard Shine

authorHOUSE®

AuthorHouse™
1663 Liberty Drive
Bloomington, IN 47403
www.authorhouse.com
Phone: 833-262-8899

Published by AuthorHouse 05/27/2022

ISBN: 978-1-6655-5815-0 (sc)
ISBN: 978-1-6655-5816-7 (e)

CONTENTS

CHAPTER 1: STOP THE KILLING

CHAPTER 2: THE TRUTH IS

CHAPTER 3: A LIFETIME DETT

CHAPTER 1
Stop The Killing

STOP THE KILLING
1/020

This land of so called liberty
is dyne from the lack of unity
stop the killing so much
royal blood we are spilling.

How can we stop the killing
of white on black crime
when we can't stop the killing of our own kind.

Evil is all around us and
it's killing us everywhere
we have to keep ourselves-awake
we can die any day out here I got to pray
Just to stay, we have to find a better way.

How can we stop the killing
of white on black crime
when we can't stop the killing
of our own kind.

OPEN YOUR MIND
7/021

Turn that liquor bottle loose
put your time to some good use
stop your fighting stop the shooting
stop the killing royal blood is spilling.

This is your time stop killing your kind
open your mind, it's your time.

We close our minds to what we see
a world of pain a world of hate a world of poverty
use your time more likely
make some time then take that time
put it on line, with your mind more wisely
we, gotta stop killing royal blood is spilling.

This is your time stop killing your kind
wake up your mind this is your time
open your mind, and shine.

THE TRUTH IS (PT2)
7/021

Have you ever seen such a sight?
where the education of a nation
becomes the foundation of corruption
overnight.

The truth is the light and
everyday we fight
the truth supposed to be the light
to keep down the fight.

Have you ever seen such a sight?
temporary fools from temporary fights
running from the blame showing us no shame
everybody wants to play the bad game
but nobody wants a bad name.

The truth is the light and
everyday we do fight when
the truth supposed to be the light to help
keep down the fight.

ANOTHER GHETTO GAME
7/021

The slum can make you thin
the slum can make you fat
the slum can turn you into a cold-hearted brat.

Reaching for the fame
running from the blame
showing us no shame is
just another ghetto game.

Don't knock this glory here comes another story
evil is his name
the devil and his game
hell has no ferry like evil has no shame. and

We are reaching for his fame
running from the blame and
showing no shame is just
another ghetto game.

THIS IS SCARY
6/021

What does it take to change the minds
of people who condon evil
we got an issue we got a gun
you kill my daughter and I'll kill your son
this, is scary.

Your going down town
they put you underground
where stand your ground is holding you down
everybody got a bomb we can all die any day
some of us want to live some of us don't
some of us die for a piece of the pie
what does it take to change the minds that hate
and how much longer will it escalate this is scary.

We got an issue we got a gun
this is scary Mr. Kerry
this is scary miss Cherry and
as, for me and Miss Mary, this is scary.

A DISGRACE
7/020

Are you satisfied in your life and time?
with all the hurt you find
somethings in life can hurt like hell
look like hell even smell like hell, as if
We all died and went to hell.

And it's a disgrace
the way we waste God's grace
it's just not fair if it were not for his grace
none of us would be here.
He can destroy man with just one plan and
this whole land, I can feel him and I adore him
because he's not like man. and

It's a disgrace
the way we waste God's grace
it's all in my ear, all in the air, and it's just not fair
if it were not for grace none of us would be here.

THIS LIVING GAME
7/021

In this living game it seems we find a way to
take what is good and make it bad
we even find a way to
take what's wrong and make things worse.

In this living game we play
in this living game we pay
in this living game I pray.

The truth is the light
there is no wrong without right
God is day the devil is in the night
2 wrongs don't make one right
it only stirs up another big fight.

In this living game we play
in this living game they say
in this game we all gotta pay, so
in this living game I pray.

MAKE THAT CHANGE
7/021

On their air we choke
trust becomes a joke
everybody seems to be Hating and
all they want is another smoke.

We have to make the change
that we wish to be
we have to be that change
that we all wish to see.

Our trust becomes a joke to us
we take each other's trust
we throw it under the bus and wonder
why we fuss, why we cuss, in this society.

We have to make that change
seriously this is not a game
you have to be that change
that you want to see.

MIRROR OF AMERICA (PT3)
6/020

We got guns we got schemes
we got children without dreams
crying please and I can't breathe
we don't want to end up in a deep freeze.

In this mirror of America
we been moving on for so long
we been moving strong, yet so wrong.

We got people dyne because of their color
we got people dyne because of their money and
some of them commit murder
just to be funny.

In this mirror of America
we been moving on for so long
in this mirror of America
We are moving, so strong, yet so wrong.

YOU CAN'T STOP ME
4/021

I am a struggler
I am not a smuggler
I was not born to be a thug
I am not searching for any drug.

I just want to be
who I was born to be I just want to be me and
you can't stop me.

It's my reality to know who I am
I just want to be wise I just want to realize and
keep my eyes on the prize
I'm nobody's thug and I don't need anybody's drug.

I just want to be
who I was born to be I just want to be me
that's who I intend to be and
you can't stop me.

THEY NEVER DIE
7/021

The rich the poor the young and
the old their heart and souls
the youth and their goals.

In a world where spirits fly
in a world where spirits cry
living in a world of spirits that never die.

They have roots in this society
spirits never die
some are none God fearing
some are double devil daring like the games that
left Jerome at home alone in a long syndrome.

In a world where spirits fly
in a world where spirits lie
living in a world of spirits and they never die.

WHO WE ARE
7/021

They seem to make the ghetto
worse than it has to be
when it's up to us to be fair
then it's up to us to show care.

It's up to us because
they don't care what we go through
less more what we been through and
They don't care who we are.

Death or history is no mystery
jail is a no-good place
the mind is terrible thing to waste
evil is nothing good to see
prison ain't no place to be. so

It's up to us to share it's up to us to care because
they don't care what we go through
less more what we see they could care less
who we are less more who we be.

THE CHALLENGE
7/021

Here in poverty where your big gun
is bigger than the next one and
The next one is bigger than any gun.

Living here on earth
this is the challenge this is your case
living on this earth, you must find your place.

Down here in poverty
where most of us cannot see
there is no unity just a trick society and
you wish someone could set you free
from this trickoy.

Living here on earth this is your challenge
this is your case you must find your
rightful place, amongst this human race.

JUST LIKE SATAN
7/020

These are the days and
these are our waves of difficult times
if it ain't the black then it's the white
no one wants to see the light.

A lot of us are living
not enough of us are giving
too many are just like Satan
So many of us are Hatten.

Satan ain't your best Satan ain't no guess
Satan, is your test one hell of a mess and
I really do believe this world has been deceived.

A lot of us are living
not enough of us are giving and
so many of us are just like Satan
too many of us are Hatten.,

HAND OF THE KLAN
8/021

A society of no mercy
a society of no shame
so I just keep hopping
keep my ears and eyes open.

The hand of the Klan
still destroys the black man and
how the black man mark the Klan.

Because of our gibberish conversations
I have to keep my eyes wide open
when one bad man goes down
it won't be long before another comes around
because of the way we treat one another
we must now be aware of each other.

The hand of the Klan destroys the black man and
Now the black man mark the Klan.

THEY DON'T PRAY
8/021

Damn you, names are no good games
no good games are ghetto games
we need to be someone who's fair
We need to be someone who cares.

They don't pray all they do is play
I don't play all I do is pray and I'm
looking for someone to pray with while
they're looking for someone to play with.

Holding their gibberish conversations even
the hippest chicks turn into hypocrites
with their damn you, games so full of no good names.

They don't pray all they do is play
I don't play all I do is pray and I'm
looking for someone to pray with while
they're looking for someone to play with.

FUSS AND FIGHT (PT2)
8/021

When your world crumbles down
that's not the time to play around
they got all this room to hate and
can't find the time to make it wait.

They don't wanna read
they don't wanna write
all they wanna do is fuss and fight.

I was released in a land that I did not know
so, I kept wishing and I kept hopping
until the day I heard someone say
to pray is your way to shine
it's the light for all souls and minds. but

They don't wanna pray and
they don't wanna write
all they wanna do is fuss and fight.

PREDICAMENT
8/021

Who's that face in the crowd
who's that acting mighty proud
with their heads stuck in a cloud
saying nothing, talking, loud.

How did we get in this predicament?
How did we get into this jam?
we pretend that God is dead so
we don't have to give a damn.

Who's that making mothers cry
who's that making fathers cry
the way we make our brothers die.

How did we get in this predicament?
how did we get into this jam?
living like God is dead
so we don't have to give a damn.

THIS HUMAN RACE
8/021

So, the number 1 stunners
become the number 1 slayers
slayers of their so, called players and
they have been so busy destroying their minds.

To build your own place
this is what you have to face
trying to keep the pace
in this human race.

They been so busy destroying each other
they are too busy deceiving their kind
only the bigger man has the upper hand and
only the bigger man knows where he stands.

In order to build your own place
this is what we all must face
trying to keep up with the pace
in this human race.

POOR PEOPLE VALLEY
3/021

Living in the poor people valley
we just do what we can for as long as we could
no matter how bad, no matter how good.

We are having a rally
in the poor people valley and
if no one is for the good
we can imitate our neighborhood.

If you keep on thinking right and
do this with all your, might
there'll come a day you'll see the light and
if you're brave enough to see it
then be brave enough to be it. so

We are having a rally
down in the poor people valley and
no matter how bad no matter how good
we just imitate our neighborhood.

YOUNG MIND SHINE

I don't know what you been reading
I don't know what you are feeling.

These words were design
to mentor the mind
from musical mentors, let the young mind shine.

In a world full of fantasy
we feel the good we see the bad
of all nations as a man think so is he
specially when he is in misery so
I don't know what you been thinking
I don't know what you've been drinking.

These words were design
to mentor the mind to the young mind be kind
from musical mentors to the musical mind
let the young mind shine.

ONLY THE WISE
7/021

We play some sad ghetto games
we use some foul ghetto names
it seems the system is design
to unrelax our minds.

Only the wise will rise
only the wise will realize
only the wise will survive.

This life can be for the better
this life can be for the worse
this system was designed to destroy your mind
so we can't leave what's negative behind.

Only the wise will rise
only the wise will open their eyes
only the wise will realize and
only the wise will survive.

TODAY'S SOCIETY
7/021

In today's society there is
nothing but the quickness
nothing but the sickness
nothing but the wickedness in today's society.

You can lose more than you can afford to
by biting off more than you can chew
we all have our doubt when things don't work out and
that's what this society seems to be all about.

In today's society there is
nothing but the quickness
nothing but the wrong and that don't take long
don't forget the homeless
nothing but the sickness and
nothing but the wickedness in today's society.

I MADE IT

I made it through that silly mess
I made it I passed the test
I made it through that craziness
now I need a rest.

Playing super sad ghetto games where
some of pick and choose to live
some of us chose to die
some of us pick and choose the truth
some of us chose to lie.

I made it through this silly mess
I made it I passed the test
I made it through what was, so dangerous
now I deserve a rest.

MINDS THAT HATE (PT2)
8/021

They don't read they don't write
all they do is fuss and fight and
I have reasons to believe
this whole world has been deceived.

Hell has room for worse
we have no time to wait
from evil minded people we are
dealing with minds that hate.

War pain and poverty all at the same time
all in a modern kind of pace here's where
every ghetto carries low mercy
without any grace.

Hell has room for worse
we have no room to wait
from evil minded people we are
dealing with minds that hate.

WHY NOT
8/021

If the world does not hear
if the world is not fair and
the world does not care why not.

Let us share a little love
let us show a little light
when we share our love
we can show what is right.

Some men see things as they are and
they ask why, but me
I can see where love is needed and I ask why not
If every possibility can live within our dreams why not.

Let us all share a little love
we all must show some kind of light
when we share our love
we can show what we know is right.

THE WORLD'S DESTINY
8/021

If it's for me to see
if it's for you to be then
it's for us to be all we can be in this society.

Whatever it is you see
there is no mystery for we are the key
to this world's destiny.

We as elders let's stop doing
as we choose to
we as elders let start doing
what we see needs to be done
if it's for me to see if it's for you to be.

Whatever it is you see
there is no mystery for we are the key
to the world's destiny.

THE DEVIL'S PLAYGROUND (PT2)
8/021

A little education can go a long way
but the wrong education
can destroy a whole nation as
we fly so high staring into the devil's eye.

The evilest playground that's ever been found
the evilest playground around is
the devil's playground. and

I have reason to believe by satan
we all have been received and
I have reason to believe by satan
We all have been deceived.

The evilest playground that's ever been found and
the evilest playground
that has ever been around is
the devil's playground.

THE BIGGER MAN
8/021

We are walking on a rafter
enjoying life in every laughter
here now and ever after still we are
destroying the black man and we need a better plan.

May the bigger man stand
the bigger man knows how to keep down violence
The bigger man knows how to prerelease silents.

For so many days from so many ways came
too many early graves and
too many evil deeds got done it's like
walking and laughing on a roof on a rafter
here now and forever after.

May the bigger man stand
the bigger man knows how to
keep down violence and
the bigger man knows how to prerelease silents.

WE SHALL BE FREE
9/021

You and me we both shall be free
micshell lee and me
yes we shall be free.

Even if it's still alive we will survive
even if it survive we will be alive and
we will be free from mental slavery.

If you like spice darken the rice
just ask anybody they will tell you twice
I'm the only one who will treat you nice.

Just put your trust in me and
we both shall be free
micshell lee and me yes we shall be free.

MENTAL SLAVEY
9/021

We are stuck in mental violence
we are stuck in mental slavey
we dress so fly we drive so high
we drove straight into a DUI.

We are still stuck in mental violence
we are still stuck in mental slavey and
it's not worth the time it wasn't worth it then and
it's not worth it now getting locked down like a slave
going down into an early grave.

If we are stuck in mental violence
then we are stuck in mental slavey and
those who are into mental violence
needs to come out from mental slavey.

MESSENGER OF MISERY
9/90

I am the messenger
I am not the misery
I'm just the messenger as you can see,
I was born in poverty.

Quarter pounder plain
snow turns into rain
as a messenger of misery you got to face the blame.

We hope you don't wakeup living in a breakup and
I'm not trying to be the misery you see because
life for me can also be such a mystery and
it's better instead when we do not spread
such a messed-up head. so that

Quarter Pounder plain
snow turns into rain, sorta sound the same
so don't be ashamed
the messenger of misery has got to face the blame.

THE RICH IN YOU
9/91

Anytime you're feeling blue
here comes someone more poor than you
anytime your heart gets smart
Here comes a heart as smart as you.

So anytime you're feeling blue
the rich in you lights the sky so blue
as the rich get richer in you.

So poorman keep your spirits up to
whenever you think of going to the bank
there is someone who does more than think and
that someone could be you too.

So anytime you're feeling blue
if the poor is you instill light in you
the rich in you lights the sky so ture
there is rich in you like the clear sky blue
as the rich get richer in you.

A STRANGE PLACE
12/98

This world is a strange place
it can put a frown upon your face
it keeps a space that can't be replace
the lives we need are the lives we waste.

I'm so tired I want to try
I'm so sick I want to fly
I'm so happy I want to die.

Some hatchets are too big for barry
while others are too big to berry
so barry gave his to mary
old habits are hard to break slavey ain't no mistake.

This world is a strange place
we heed to the race
where there's not enough space
the lives we need are the lives we waste
my God this world is a strange place.

RUBY TUESDAY
12/98

Here comes a cool day in the news
here comes a new day win or lose
ruby tuesday ruby chose
ruby chase away the tuesday blues.

It was a new day in the news
every tuesday she paid her dues
no a monday ruby moves
she refuse to buy my shoes.

Ruby tuesday ruby tues
it's a cool day on the news
ruby tuesday ruby chose
ruby chase away the tuesday blues.

SUPPRESS
9/021

You got to know when to hold'em
you got to know when to fold'em
you got to suppress this, you got to surpass that.

Somethings come as a test
somethings happen for the best
someone has to clear this mess
somethings you have to suppress.

Somebody needs a chill pill
some of us need to bestill
some of us can't afford a pill less more bestill
Emanuel 9 was a sign to stop the killing of our kind.

Somethings come as a test
somethings happen for the best
somethings need to be address,
somethings you have to suppress.

LINGER LONGER ROAD
9/021

There's no one to linger
no one longer down
this linger longer road.

No one lingers longer
than I do with this linger longer load
no more linger no more longer no more road and.

No more lingering
no more longer on this
linger long road
no one lingers no more load down
this road.

MENTICIDE
9/021

Reality is your destiny
it's what you hear it's what you see
reality is what we be and too much
tv can cause more mystery.

It's menticide somewhat like suicide
a proper killing of the inside
it's in your mind, it's in your ear everyday of the year.

Social media is like a cigar is to cigarettes
once you get addicted there is no rest
it's in your ear it's in your hair
the end is near and here comes the fear.

It's menticide somewhat like suicide
a proper killing of your inside
all in your mind all in your hair the end is near
Here comes the fear everyday of the year.

SATURDAY NIGHT
7/85

It was saturday night
the moon was bright
no need to feel so uptight.

Many gather around to hear
good sounds in the atmosphere
a friendly smile face to face
show no worries show no trace
it's the night for you to be happy in reality.

Fairest wheels going around
you had to seek for what you found
mary hurry don't you fall go head on have a ball
happy in reality you see
you see
you see.

A BETTER PEOPLE

And it hit me like a vision
I'm suppose to be on a mission
we got to do some good in our neighborhood
first we'll clear our minds of evil
then we'll stomp out all evil it's the only way
to become a better people.

Let's look at motherhood
it don't always look so good
brotherhood is misunderstood
fatherhood not all of us should
if we love our neighborhood
we gotta get out and do some good
we gotta get out and try
just don't live here and die.

First we'll clear our minds of evil and
we'll clear our hearts of all evil then
we'll save our children from evil
It's the only way to become a better people.

GETAWAY
9/021

The richman's heaven
is the poor man's hell as in
The rich man's trash is a poor man's sale.

As you live today it's a game they play
never work to stay if you have to work then
work to get away.

When your flying on a dangerous
flight at night
when you're working at a dangerous
job site.

That's the game they play and
in this game we have to pay so
do like sticky say, never work to stay
if you have to work then work to get away.

HE HAS GIVEN
8/97

So you say there is so much bad in your life
all that's bad makes you sad and
all the love that you never had ''well''.

There is a gift that God has given us all
because he rather see you stand
than to see you fall.

His gift to you is all in your life and
that one life is meant to be a light
he knows to gain is your delight
he helps us live by faith and not by sight.

When by the side so many fall
he can see you standing tall so
the gift he has given comes to us all because
he would rather see you stand than to see you fall.

IN HELL
9/021

Here in hell there is a way to pay
so watch what you do
watch what you say night and day.

Over here it's call the ghetto
it seems no one wants to let go
that's where Fred hit his head
that's where the living seems dead and
the dead seems to come alive
over here there is no feeling
over here there is no healing.

Here in hell there is a way to pay
so watch how you play
there's a way to say there's a way to pray so
watch what you say every night and day.

NO GUARANTEES
9/021

I don't chase behind heffers
I don't hang around hoodlums
their too busy wasting their time, and
time has no guarantees.

Our time is in the making
are we just taking out time
minds are surely wasting,
are we truly wasting our time?

Whatever goes on today
there is no way we can say
where there's a will there is no way
we have no time for mystery, time has no guarantees.

Our time is in the making
are we truly taking out time
are we truly wasting our minds
time has no guarantees
are we truly wasting our time?

BE CAREFUL
9/021

Welcome to America
welcome to this hell just don't leave the light on
hell is in America and America is in hell.

Be careful in what you fear
be careful of what you hear
be careful of what you do,
it will come back to you.

Isn't it great you're never too late
isn't it great I mean all eight
pushing you through another gate and
Whatever you contribute to is usually not great.

Be careful of what you fear
be careful of what you hear
be careful of the things you do
they will come back to you.

A WONDERFUL WAY
9/021

When it looks like evil and it sounds like evil
when it's hell like the wave
that's just like evil racing to the grave.

It would be in a wonderful way
if I get the time to see the day
it would be in a wonderful day
if we bow our heads and pray.

When your life has darkness and
all you can find is hate online
just give your heart and life to God,
he will give you peace of mind.

It would be in a wonderful way
if we could find the time to pray
it would be in a wonderful day
if this whole nation would say,
let us bow our heads and pray.

THE EVIL OF VIOLENCE
9/021

Just like a phillapean so full and plain
pain hate and poverty no love in your name
no love in your heart no love in your game
you walk this road and carry this load of pain.

The violence of every evil
is the evil of the people so
I break the code of silence by
resisting the violence of evil.

Hate pain and poverty
when this lives amongst our people
we all live unwell evil gets the best of people and
my people are now in hell. so

The violence of every evil
is the evil of the people and somehow
I break the code of silence
by resisting the violence of evil.

YOU HAVE NO SHAME
9/021

We must stop satan and his army of evil
love is an emotion love has a name
love is not a gamble, love is not a game.

With that lie in your game
you lie to the world in Jesus name
you criticize my people in all their pain and
you think nothing of it, because you have no shame.

Evil in our lives you see lead our minds to misery
we place upon our kind
we spend more time for a white crime
then we spend for our own kind.

With that lie in your game
you lie to the world in Jesus name
you criticize my people in all of their pain and
you think it's funny cause you have no shame.

CHAPTER 2

The Truth Is

THE PROMISE CHILD
9/021

We got troubles we got pain
we got struggles we got no shame
even though we live in the shadows of death
someday you will lead and
this world will come through.

The promise child
from the promised land
for the promise children we stand.

A new breed of evil has been born amongst us
perhaps you will lead us into a better way to live
Hopefully you will teach us a better reason to give.

The promise child
from the promised land
for you we promise to lend our hand
for the promise children we stand
on this promised land.

WHAT'S HAPPENING
10/021

So many people too many dare
so many want to use you
so many want to abuse you and
I heard someone cry, too many ways to die.

So what's happening is the same old shame
just playing the game still happens here today and
the same foul name feels the same.

Too many gangsters too many guns
we don't always get the best but
we sure can make a mess and
you only get so much time to rest.

So what's happening? my guess
the same old shame playing your name
still happens here today and the same old
violence that used to be, still goes on today.

A NEW MEANING
10/019

When it comes to words to live by
we all don't see eye to eye and
there goes another lie from days gone by.

You have to practice your living
give your life a new meaning
show how you learned to maintain and
your living will not be in vain.

Our ancestors were queens and kings
we are their offsprings
they are not going to pave the way alone and
all the rest of us go free, there is a lesson here
for everyone and here is one from me.

You have to practice your living
give your life a new meaning
teach your brain to sustain and
your living will not be in vain.

A SET UP
4/013

They can't pin me for any robbery
they can't pin me for any murder
they can't pin me for any child support so
I'll meet you at the basketball court.

It's a setup and the plan is to
keep you locked up
it's a setup in the clothes we wear
it's a setup in the way we care.

You stole a car in one short trip
it turn out to be an unmarked whip
we got more than many fears
we got less than health care and never enough years.

It's a setup a setup in the games we play
a setup in the words we say a setup in the clothes we wear
a setup in the music we hear, it's all a setup.

A MOTHER

Another chapter to recapture
another soul calls the here after
when a family loses someone
a mother loses her daughter a father loses his son.

Now there comes a time when we all must find
according to how we leave this world we need
some peace of mind tomorrow is not promise
today has no guarantees.

A father loses his son
life seems to have no fun
reopen another chapter another soul
calls the here after
a mother loses her daughter
a father loses his son a daughter loses her mother
we all will lose someone.

NO KIND OF MISTAKE
9/021

This is more than you can stand
this is more than you can take so
slow your role and take a break
keep on your shoes unrelax your feet
this is the truth and it doesn't sound so sweet.

This ain't no joke
this ain't no fake this kind of book
ain't no kind of mistake.

This is more than I can stand
let's go back to when we were great
to see if there was any mistake
steady your mind no time to unwine because
we spend less time for a crime
when we do it to our kind.

More than one man can stand or I can take
this ain't no joke and it takes no break
this kind of book aint, no kind of mistake.

THAT SICKENS ME
10/021

There is a new breed of evil
that is now amongst us and
that new breed is now coming down upon us and
no matter how we breed she is made of greed.

What kind of person you chose to be
what kind of future you want to see
one super sick society and that sickens me.

As in some things never change when
so many things need to be changed like
the company of thugs on your street
that's not cool and it sure ain't neat.

What kind of future you want to see
what kind of person you chose to be
one super violent sick society
and that sickens me.

BETWEEN LOVE AND HATE
10/021

The line is too thin, the line is too tight
someone open the gate, there's no time to wait
we got a mighty thin line between love and hate
when you have no issues
you quickly become an issue.

Too much hate plus too much evil equals
too many of us dyn
living like God is dead
when did we get that through our heads
now is the time there's no time to wait
we got to separate love from hate.

We got to thicken the line
it's gonna take some weight
someone open the gate, we got no time to wait
we got a mighty thin line
between love and hate.

FOUL LANGUAGE
10/021

It's a setup from the past
it's a setup for the future
they set us up for their sake so
we all won't awake and see how it kills you and me.

We use it when we are sad
we use it when we are happy
we use it when we are mad, foul language.

Some of us say it to our fathers
some of us say it to our brother
they even say it to their mother and
we keep killing each other, when does it end.

We say it when we feel good
we say it when we feel bad
we say it when we are angry
we say it when we are sad, even gwen got her's in
when does it end?

RICH MAN'S WORLD
10/021

It makes me want to holla
so much evil so many kinds
so many people all different minds and
the police decrease the peace in our daily lives.

It makes me want to holla
the way the poor gets mistreated
in this rich man's world.

If we are the world
we can give our lives a new meaning
if we are the world then let's stop hating each other and
let the good deeds of our ancestors live in our daily lives.

It makes we want to holla
the way the poor gets mistreated
it makes me want to holla the way people are
gun down in this rich man's world.

THOSE WHO ARE KIND
10/021

The eyes of war are upon you
be kind man take the mask from
your face and face man be kind man
keep the mask near your face just in case.

Don't turn toward crime
keep your peace of mind
heaven holds a place for those who are kind.

The eyes of evil are watching as
their greed becomes more of a need
too many thugs too many guns so now you
must be one of the best to come out from amongst this mess.

Just don't turn toward crime
keep your ever-loving peace of mind
heaven holds a place for those who are kind.

TO ALL MANKIND
10/021

There was a time when I was blind and
could not keep up so I stayed behind
until I opened up my mind to the ways
of mankind.

To all mankind this is for your time
this is for all the hurt you find
seeking from the reflection in your eyes
it's about our time to rise.

This life seems like a trip, this trip is my life
for some of us it's a long one
for others it's a short one and we have yet
to live like brothers and see as family.

To all mankind this is for your mind
and all the hurt you find we can see
it's no surprise from that reflection in your eyes
it's about our time to rise.

OUR SORROW
10/021

Why do we get stomped by police?
they don't see us as humans
they only see wild and vicious animals
so, they think in wild and vicious ways.

Here comes a demon kicking and screaming
we're going to turn our sorrow into pure gold and
make you reap just what you sow.

When it comes to deep down daily demons
bad cops always fit in
a positive mind can product a gold mind and
give our lives new meaning
when you do evil deeds you sow bad seeds.

Where is that demon kicking and screaming
we're going to turn our sorrow into pure gold
and make you reap just what you sow.

YOUR SOUL THE SIGN (PT1)
10/021

You say you are my brother and
you care to show your leaning but
all you ever show is a gun or a knife
a way to take another brother's life.

Open up your mind
don't keep killing your kind
We gotta find a way to, feed your soul the sign.

No one could see your knife
you called your brother's wife, you deceived him
you took his life and you did this thing twice
we have to find a way to bring some love here today.

Open up your mind
don't keep killing your kind you got to find
some kinda way, to feed your soul the sign.

THE PAST
11/021

We are studying the past
in our modern city class and
we are keeping it going fast
violence moves through modern minds
trouble is moving through different times.

The past is moving fast and it has a way to last
the past don't leave us last
it moves into a higher class.

In our modern schools
are modern city blues
bugs are in your face, people are on your case
you can't find a decent place.

The past is moving fast it has a way to last
the past don't always leave so fast
it moves on to a higher class.

WEBSITE LINE
11/014

Be aware it's that time of the year
somethings just might disappear
if you drink from a bottle of wine
you'll never know what you might find.

This world is our only world
this world is in disguise
a world designed from the website line
you'll never know what you might find.

I heard there is something wicket in the water
the wicket gets a ticket from bohicket's daughter
and there's an act of a man from the klu klux klan
the most vicious man on God's land.

This world is our only world
a world so full of disguises
a world designed from a website line
you'll never know what you

SATAN IS THE MAN
11/021

Another fools another one
another high school another gun
people cannot live without people
but we can surely live without evil.

Who holds the plan only the klann and
Satan is the man
who holds the hand of the klann.

This is no debate so let's keep it straight
the system is not fair and America is not great
she has a demon one that has no shame
As a messenger of misrey I have to say the same.

Who holds the plan the klu klux klan
and Satan is the man,
who holds the hand of the klann.

BUILD YOUR NEST
11/021

Evil comes from the past
evil has a way to last and
as long as we don't care,
our evil ain't going nowhere.

Build your nest do your best
build your nest without wickedness
build your nest.

The past is in the future,
as the future comes from the past
those who come from the bad part past
can be bad for your future and long as
we say we don't care, our future ain't going nowhere.

Build your nest do your best
build your nest not wickedness and
do your best to seek righteousness
as you build your nest.

REPRESENTATIVES
11/021

They damn you if you do
they damn you if you don't
most of us we live for the good and
just like the wise we shall rise.

We are representatives of all people
we represent our good
while others represent their evil.

There is some good in this hood and
we represent for that good
while others are showing off, we are the ones
who represent our reputation
for the hurt and pain of this nation.

We are representatives for our people
we represent our good
while others represent their evil
not all of us live for our people
there are those who live for evil.

GOD'S NOT DEAD
11/021

Sin is not a friend sin comes from within
we must be born again sin wants your soul
sin wants your time, sin is in the mind.

God, is not dead but we are dying
planes crash instead of flynn and
it looks like we are dying.

You say you love your people but
all you ever do is hurt the ones who love you
loving in what you hear and living in what you wear
watch whatever it is you do, it will come back to you.

God, is not dead but we are dying
some of us love his truth some of us are lien
airplanes crash instead of flynn and
it looks like we are dying.

THE TRUTH IS HERE
11/021

We are living in hell
like no one can tell 'O' well
another one steals a sale as
another one lands in jail and.

The truth is here this is the year
the time has come let go of the gun
the truth is here, it's on the one.

And then when I was young
a well dress lie came rushing by
it seem the only way to stay in check
was to give each other the lowest respect
the kind we all can live without now finally.

This is the year the truth is here
and every day it gets more clear
the truth is here let go of the gun
the truth is here, for everyone.

IN THE HOOD
11/021

Troubles are in the hood
we got the bad and we got the good
we are full with all our should nots and
all the things that you should.

I remember there was a time when
they would only shoot at night
now they don't care how wrong or right
they'll shoot you in broad daylight.
troubles in the hood can lead you straight to jail and
it can come from running behind the wrong dress tail.

Troubles are in the hood
we got the bad and we got it good
so don't get caught up in this hood
with everything that's not so good.

LET'S DO SOME GOOD
11/021

We got a thin line between life and death
we got a thin line to the very last breath
and between love and hate
that's an act of our mental state.

The truth is here the truth is clear
it's in the hood everybody get out
let's do some good.

If there is anybody here without a care
we got, old folks are out here living in fear
young people are out here who don't care and
the truth is not for fun, everybody rising a gun
and everyone under the sun got one.

The truth is in your neighborhood
everybody get out do what you should
the truth is clear and in your hood
everybody get out, let's do some good.

FOR HUMANITY
11/021

For the betterment of humanity
our minds are important
our time is important
our lives are important, this must be true.

There is a sick side of America
that wants to destroy the positive side
when they connect themselves with
every part of the bad that comes from the past but
for the betterment of humanity this must be true.

It is important that we better ourselves
so we can better our neighborhood
so we can better our community
so we can build a better society for humanity.

THE FUTURE PAST
11/021

Some more evil for more evil
deliver our people from the fruits of evil
chaos for the future, chaos from the past,
we got a future just as bad as the past.

It's the future past it's moving fast
as we drag our future back into the past.

A future as bad as the past
no matter how slow or fast
we take the past and make it last
turn to love and it won't be ashamed
turn to love and it won't be a pain.

It's the future past and
it's moving real fast as we drag
our own future back into the past.

YOUR SOUL THE SIGN (PT2)
11/016

No man can live by bread alone
we need something to hold us
we need something to console us
We need to feed our souls.

To all mankind it's about that time
you need your soul we need your mind,
you need to feed your soul the sign.

When we listen it's a blessing
just to find out what we been missing
only a few can pursue all the troubles we go through,
We are living in a time where
we can't find peace of mind.

To all mankind it's about that time
show your seed show the sign, you need your soul
we need your kind, you need to feed
your soul the sign.

TAKE ME THERE

You been walking this road of life and
this ain't living 50 years of life and
all the troubles we are giving,
I feel a storm coming on and a strong one.

Take me there where the people care
take me there where the air is clear,
where the world is fair take me there.

When I always had less
when I never had the best and they abused my name
you took my little spark of hope and fan it into a flame,
when my future seemed unclear you were there.

Take me there where the people care
take me there where the air is clear,
where the world is fair
where the people care, take me there.

WHERE WE BELONG
12/021

Where we belong
we don't wanna do wrong
care is where care is here
care is where we belong.

There was a man who loved his son
he is now in pursuit of a gun and
we all thought he loved someone
we who all believes in God even though the way gets hard,
no one cares to be fair and
we, all got a cross to bear.

Where we belong
we don't wanna do no wrong where we belong
somebody help me sing this song
care is care care is here and
care is where we belong.

MEANING IN YOUR LIFE
12/021

This is your time somewhere in your mind
you are the man to give us a hand
we need your help to heal this land.

This is your time
put some peace in your mind
just put away the knife and
put some meaning in your life.

This is your life be what you want to be
smile and tell the world you are free
this is your time where is your mind
whenever you waste your time
right along goes your mind.

Just put it in your mind this is your time
to stop the killing of your kind, let's put
away the guns and put away the knife and
let's, put some meaning in your life.

EVIL
8/91

Evil we live evil we give
evil we share because evil don't care
an evil stain upon the brain
brings about an evil game.

Evil grows like never before
in so many ways you cannot ignore
evil is the name evil is the game,
evil of a redeye flame, we and evil are about the same
evil, in the place to be, brings out all our misery.

Evil we live evil we give
evil we dare because evil don't care
evil lie an evil eye we must somehow make evil die
to some it's a game they should be the blame
retaliate, is the game and evil has no shame.

OUR REAL ENEMY
11/021

When the mind get so blind until
you can't help but kill your kind
that's when it's time to wake up and see
who is your real enemy.

Lord you are the eyes
for those who cannot see
Lord you are the mind
for those who are not free and
Lord you are the ear for those who cannot hear.

You are the sight we cannot see
your love is no mystery
you com my nerve when I disagree and
it's time that we wake up and see
who is our real enemy.

HIP IN THE HOOD
12/021

Foul minds and corrupt times
reality is our tree reality and what we see,
many things we think are hip in the hood
turns out to be no good.

What's so hip about jail time
what's so hip about an evil mind
what's so hip about beating up your mother,
what's so hip about killing your brother.

Reality is our tree reality is what we be
it's who we are, it's what we see
a foul mind is the corrupt kind, and
you're so hip in the hood.

What's so hip about stealing a car
what's so hip about smoking a cigar
what's so hip about beating on your wife,
what's so hip about taking her life, hip in the hood.

CAN A MAN
12/021

Here is where they call me brother
here is where they don't mean it and
the only way out of this hell
is to step right into heaven.

Can a man count to eleven
before he gets to seven
can a man transform hell into heaven.

Who is your brother
can a man tell, when he's in hell
a Godly seed was planted into each of us
but because of what others say,
so many take theirs and throw it away and
the only way out of hell is to step right into heaven. so

Can a man count to eleven
before he gets to seven and can a man
take this hell and transform it into heaven.

THE MINDS OF MEN
12/021

This is the year of the trouble man
you can tell as he takes the stand
no ones gonna heal his land
man becomes another soul unease.

Hate becomes the minds of men
like so many others those who rather
die like fools than to live like brothers.

Evil is still on capital hill and it's not gonna bestill
another fool kills someone,
we all got some God in us we got some evil to
which one will you let get the best of you.

Hate becomes the minds of men
for so long like so many others
men who rather die like fools,
than to live as brothers.

TO EVERY STORY
12/021

There is a man with a gun
now in pursuit and on the run
there was a man who loved his son
he's now in pursuit of a gun.

There is two sides to every face
there are two sides to every case
there are two sides to every glory,
there are two sides to every story.

There is no time for us to wait
we got a thin line between love and hate
the evil of violence is the unbalance of people
while the absence of silence bears the weight of all evil.

There is two sides to every face
there are two sides in every case
there are two sides to every glory,
and there's two sides to every story.

FIGHT THE POWER
12/021

You were born and raised in living hell
trouble is all around you people are everywhere
we call ourselves raising children
instead we end up raising hell.

We kill our father we kill our mother
we kill our sister we kill our brother,
we can't fight the power so we kill each other.

Our freedom of speech
becomes freedom of death
we can't fight the power so we do the first thing
that comes to mind and that's called kill your kind.

So we kill our father we kill our sister
we kill our own mothers and brother
we can't fight their power
so we kill each other.

KENTUCKY'S KINGDOM
12/021

There is no sky without a ground
there is no up without a down
there is no black without a brown
There is no city without a town.

Somebody's town is going down
somebody's town is tumbling down
somebody's town is gonna hit the ground.

Now you won't go back home
now you won't go back to work
now you won't go back to evil and
you won't go back to business as usual.

Somebody's town is coming down
somebody's town is gonna hit the ground
somebody's town is gonna frown because,
somebody's kingdom is tumbling down.

STOP THE KILLING (PT2)
12/021

We have no time to lose our minds
we have no time for booze
It's a new day, we need a new way.

On another day and
it's a time a new wave of crime
we need to find a new way, to stop killing our kind.

We are on another day
another game is what we play
london bridge is falling down,
you got no time to pray, do as Simon say.

It's a time a new wave of crime
and I don't mean turpentine
we got to find some new way
to stop the killing of our kind.

UNITED STATES OF DRUGS
12/021

Who is your doctor the bigger the headache
the bigger the pill
the bigger the melarial the higher the hill.

Who is your doctor
is it doctor oxy is it doctor contin,
prescription thugs under the rugs
in the United States of drugs.

A doctor sits in jail
for making the wrong drug sale now
he can't heal a witch's tail,
less more keeping you out of jail and
prescription weights for many, of days.

The bigger the melarial the bigger the thrill
prescription thugs
under prescription rugs
in the United States of prescription drugs.

LAND OF THE LIVING

In this land of the living we try our best
to transform hell into heaven and
hell has been hell for who knows how long.

This is the land
these are the hands
heal every woman heal every man
in this land of the living.

In the memories of my mind
you told me this is my time
you told me to be kind and
when I feel like I'm falling apart
I keep your word close to my heart.

This is the land these are the hands
heal every woman heal every man
heal this land yes we can
heal this land of the living.

READ MY MIND (PT2)
12/021

When you feel so unkind and
need to feed your soul the sign
go ahead and read my mind.

These are my words by richard
this is my mind by shine
go ahead read my book, read my mind.

Oldman brad he's still sad
because of the love he never had and
the power is in his soul
the power is in your time, the power is in the sign,
the power within your mind.

These are my words by richard
this is my mind by shine
go ahead and read my book
it's your time to shine, read my mind.

SONGS TO WRITE
12/013

Songs of you songs of me and
how we want our lives to be.

Songs to write I could sleep last night
I got songs to write
if the world is an apple let me take a bite
I got songs to write.

I got to write about the right
I got to write about the wrong and
the way we get along, how it helps me remain strong
songs of how we love, songs of how we fight, so
don't get uptight, I got songs to write.

Songs to write I couldn't sleep last night
I got songs to write
if the world is an apple let me take a bite
because I got songs to write.

BE BLESSED
10/013

All the blame all the shame
calling me out of my right name and
In this life in this game I refuse to be the same.

I change from water to flesh
sinking the hair on my chest
I change from more to less and
I would rather be blessed.

I was purple I was pink
I was every way you think
when I am down when I am out
I don't have to scream or shout,
I am not what this world is about.

I change from more I change to less
I change from less I change to best
I change from water back to flesh, and still
I would rather be blessed.

SOMEDAY
1/020

I have felt a pain that I cannot explain
the kind that puts poison in your vains
what's my name the fiery flame,
Ask me again and I'll say the same.

Some may laugh some may grin
some days I'm out some days I'm in
someday buddy I'm gonna win.

I have seen the years I have felt the tears
felt them running down my ears
I grab my seat when I'm in defeat
too many blood stains on my street.

Some may laugh some may grin
some days I'm out some days I'm in
sundays and mondays may come to an end
But someday buddy I'm gonna win.

DEMONS
1/014

They can follow you they can follow me
none of them can be captured
all of them are free in a heart so dark
where no eyes can see.

Demons fly demons lie
that's how demons get by
demons get high demons lie,
That's why demons must die.

A man can't see pass broad daylight
he end up killing his wife last night
he would've followed you he could of followed me
in a heart so dark where no eyes can see.

Demons fly everything but die, that's how demons get by
demons lie demons cry that's how demons get high and
That's why all demons must die.

ON THIS PLANET
10/015

"O" say we have come a long way
so many say we got a long way to go
so many on this planet I don't understand it
troubles are a lot and together we are not.

On this planet I don't understand it
people down here taking life for granit
take me far beyond this planet,
where there's no place to be a shame.

We use to show love but that could never last
we did not understand the past and
it goes away so fast and we all didn't do
what we could to improve our neighborhood.

And on this planet I don't understand it
people down here taking life for granit,
take me far beyond this planet
where there's no one to complain and
no way to feel the shame.

A DIFFERENCE
9/015

I'm gonna make a difference
too much negativity can kill a man
don't think it can't because it can
too many foul words has been spoken
too many good hearts have been broken.

Now is the time I'm gonna make a difference
there are some things we can change
I'm gonna make a difference, it's gonna feel real good.

I'm gonna teach on the beach
where many souls are hard to reach
I'm gonna feed the poor wipe my feet at every door
bandage their wounds where they say it's sore.

Now is my time I'm gonna make a difference
these kind of things we can change
I'm gonna make a difference and
It's gonna feel real good.

ITALIAN STREAMS

These are a few lines go run tell
we hope these few lines find you well
not in a mess but all in the flesh
and not so dangerous.

The city of dreams
becomes the city of sirens
down crystal blue italian streams.

You can be the first to know and
the last one to go or
you can be the first to show and
be the last one to know by all means.

When the city of dreams becomes a city of sirens
one thousand screams to one thousand dreams and
for all it means down crystal blue italian streams.

THE CROCKETT LIFE
10/014

I have been around for some years
I have been around I seen some tears
I worked the fields from day to day and
It's funny how money can slip away.

I was going down a crockett road
I was heading down a crockett path
I was following the crockett, life.

I thought I was cool I could be nobody's fool
that year I dropped out of high school
hanging out, all night shooting pool, until
one night I heard thunder and I began to wonder.

I was going down a crockett road
heading down that crockett path,
sharpping my pocket knife,
I was following the crockett life.

TO YOUR FUTURE

For every man for every one
for every daughter for every son
there is a certain degree to our history
when words of hate make you face reality.

Here's to your future
welcome to the rain here's to your future
welcome to the blame.

There you are where people get to judge you
by the clothes you wear
hate you for the color of your hair
knowing how much they don't care and,
The hate becomes more clear every year.

Here's to your future
welcome to the game
Here's to your future now here comes the pain.

CHAPTER 3

A LifeTime Dett

ALL THAT
5/014

Shots are being fired crooks are being hired
and a child gets caught in the crossfire
that's what I read in the news
hearts are being broken, children are being abused.

When it doesn't have to be all that
we don't need to do all that
that's not the way we should be.

And now I have to take time out
from these troubles that I find
just to ease my worried mind,
even education put in the wrong hands
can destroy a whole nation. and

It don't have to be all that
we don't need to see all that
that's not the way to be free and
that's not the way we need to be.

THIS WAY

Like a real big wheel it's a real big world
you really got to get out there
you really have to care and
we really got to get somewhere.

I believe in me and all it's gonna be
this way I won't go alone
This way my heart can stay strong.

We dress so fine in the summertime
some of us are sipping summer wine
when we have to find some kind of sign,
to keep some peace of mind, so.

I believe in you if I believe in me
and what all it's gonna be
this way we won't go alone
this way we can be strong
This way we can't go wrong, this way.

THE FINAL CALL (PT2)
1/022

There is a new American game
that's played throughout this nation and
The name of that game is a new wave of damnation.

Go ahead on have a ball
keeping it all off the wall
this one is, for you all this is the final call.

Even the rich they are evil
they want more and they need people
people can't live without people but
We sure can live without evil, and that ain't all.

Go ahead yawl have a ball
until it's all off the wall
this one here is for you all, and
This is the final call.

THE NEW JIM CROW
1/022

I got to find me an act new jack
I gotta find me a blackman
and I don't mean batman
I got to drop this crap on a blackmans back.

That's the setup bro, it's the new jim crow
you got to spend more time for the same crime.

Evil people shouldn't have a place in the future
their only place should be in the past
they crack a smile they talk a while they play
like a child, just to hide their denile.

That's the setup bro
that's the new jim crow
you got to spend more time for their crime
then you do if you kill your own kind.

MIGHTY LORD CAN
1/022

Who is the man who holds the plan
who can help you understand
who is the man who can heal this land,
the mighty Lord can.

Somewhat like the final call
no matter how tall, no matter how small
no matter how you hate it, or like it at all
who you gonna call, what are you gonna do
when 9 hundred fate trains are coming down on you.

Call on mighty Lordy
mighty Lord can
he can heal this land
mighty Lord knows the plan
the mighty Lord can.

TAKE IT FROM ME
1/022

You got the same old habits
you got the same old heart
we got the same evil minds
going around in modern times, and
you're so young, having so much fun.

Take it from me so you can be free
free from all evil free from misery
free as a fish in the sea.

As another fools another one
too many has been fooled now there's no fun
another high school under the sun
another teenager another gun and
you're so young looking for fun.

Take it from me in hopes that you see
take it from me so you can be free
free from all evil, free from misery as free as a fish in the sea

A LIFETIME DETT
6/020

What's better than deceiving
giving each other a greater reason
what's better than pushing crack
or just holding each other back.

See to it the life of your ancestors
don't let their living go in vain
be about it the life of your elders
We owe them a lifetime dett.

This is better than deceiving
like it's better to give than to receive
we have a duty an everyday season
to give each other a greater reason so
if you ain't got nothing to do, then this must be true.

See to it the life of our ancestors
don't let their living go in vain
be about it the life of your ancestors,
for their blood tears and sweat
we owe them a lifetime, dett.

WE NEED LOVE

On such a beautiful day
some other maniac pulls another crazy act
in such an ugly way and where ever
hate flows, that's the way life goes.

If we want to live together
if we want to live in peace
there is no doubt about it
We need love.

Some of our lives are long
some of our lives are short
so many lives are broken in two and
most of these things we cannot undo but.

If we want to live together we need love
if you want to live with joy and raze that baby boy
there is no doubt about it this world is overcrowded
We can't live without it, we need love.

GLADTICANE

I was walking the streets without love
I was living in the street without food to eat
and sleeping on the street is never neat so,
I know you will take away this sorrow
either today or maybe tomorrow.

Over here there is no sorrow
over here there is no shame
heaven knows your name,
heaven's gladticane.

I was running through the street
I could never stand defeat
so I learned how to hate
just like I learned how eat, so I know you can take away this sorrow,
here today or maybe tomorrow.

Over here there is no sorrow
over here there is no pain
heaven knows your name heaven's glad you came
heaven's gladticane.

HATE NEVER CHANGE
1/022

These are the chances we take
theses are the choices we make
so many roads to chose
so many ways to win or lose.

It's hard to love so you turn to hate
since it's not so hard, though it's not so great
You learn how to hate because it's not too late.

Our hate never change it stays in shame
that's what makes a conduction remain the same
love makes the world go around, but
Since hate is here, love is lost and can't be found.

It's so hard to love so you learn how to hate
since it's not too hard and you're not so great
when you learn to hate, you don't have to wait, so you
learn how to hate because it's never too late.

FOR THE YOUNG
1/022

When adversity turns away from right
to go along with the wrong while
young people are leaving here everyday
at any time and every way.

The good die young from an automatic gun
the bad die young the young die young
There is no fun just the son of a gun.

This system was set up to control
the minds of future generations
they call it the game they plant it in your brain
now here comes the message wake up and see,
What's going on, in this trick society.

The bad die young is no fun
the good die young from an automatic gun
the sad die young the young die young
There is no fun, just a son of a gun.

GOD AND MODERN MAN
1/022

In order to drive the violence
out of our neighborhoods
in order to drive this violence out of our time
we must first drive the violence
out of our hearts and minds.

God and his plan
God and modern man and
his plan is to make man understand
that all power is in his hand.

And it's not just you it's me
and it's not just me it's we
if I got a beef for you and you got one for me
then we need to swallow that beef
so we can all be free.

God and his plan God and modern man
and his plan is to make man understand
all power is in God's hand.

MODERN DAY EVIL
1/022

That's just like an evil man
you throw the brick you hide your hand
living in these last days and
you can't find any time for praise.

Modern day evil lurks around my people
with no decency no discipline we got
Modern day people, who can't get rid of evil.

We fought for the right to vote
we fought for the right to read
we fought because our rights is what we need and
now here today they wanna take it all away,
and that flag what is it good for
a flag that flew over 4 hundred years
for over 4 hundred graves of slaves.

And that's just like an evil man
throw the brick and hide your hand
modern day evil lurks around my people
modern day people, who can't get rid of evil.

THE UNSEEN HAND
1/022

They don't expect you to remember
but they won't let you forget
all the lies all the murders all the beatings
all the stealing, all the setbacks.

That's the sign of an unseen hand
that's from an unseen man
who has an unseen plan, you may never understand.

They take every cream right off the top
every cream from every crop
to take away the capacity in every society's,
they lie they steal they murder and then
they pretend nothing is wrong,
so they can keep this crime going on
they don't want any reflection of a living God in this nation.

That's the sign of an unseen hand
that comes from an unseen man and
He has an unseen plan, they don't want you to understand.

TO THE RESCUE
1/022

Here in the slum you can tell
we are trying to make heaven out of hell
but it doesn't seem to be working out too well, so.

From the less of us
comes the rest of us and
the best of us to the rescue.

You're old enough to hear
you're old enough to care
you're old enough to be fair,
but you don't understand, and you don't care.

So from the less of us
comes the rest of us and
from the rest of us comes
the best of us to the rescue.

THESE FEW LINES

I use to live in a place where
there was not much time
there was not much space
it was a trouble some time,
it was a worry some case, so

We hope these few lines find you well
it seems like we died and went to hell
everybody got their story to tell
of living under an evil spell.

We still need war on poverty
so we can set the poor people free
we must face this reality
in order to reach our destiny, and.

We hope these few lines find you well
seems like we died and went to hell
everybody got their story to tell
while living under an evil spell.

AN EARLY GRAVE (PT2)
1/022

There is a reason for living
there is a reason for leaving
there is a reason for learning, just like a reason for giving and,
I am too young to go down in an early grave.

Somethings can be said more ways than one
somethings of the young
can be done, more ways than one.

We can't keep going around
with people living on the street
animals are living in homes,
where people don't have food to eat and.

Somethings can be said more ways than one
somethings of the young
can be done more ways than one and
I am too old to be a slave and
I'm too young to go down in an early grave.

OVERCOME YOUR PAST
1/022

What becomes of a poor man's brain
when he can't get past the pain
any day can be his last day, no matter what people say
be thankful for another day.

By the renewing of your mind
you can be set free there is a pathway
to overcome your past.

And now this here is a new year
I thought we got rid of the past but
it seems like this modern day future
is just another modern day past, and
Many of us are going nowhere fast.

But by the renewing of your mind
you can be soul free this is the pathway
to overcome your past.

TOO YOUNG TO CARE
1/022

Trouble is all around you
people are everywhere
people are all around you troubles are everywhere.

You are too young to care
you are too young to see
you are too young to be, excepting drugs from an enemy.

As I was on line this was on my mind
for everyone you meet, in every group or street
may not be good company to keep
Regardless of what people say, you have to pray everyday.

You are too young to care
you're too young so behave
you are too young to go down in an early grave
you are too young to see, you are too young to be
accepting drugs from an enemy.

A SERIOUS PROBLEM
4/021

Everything that's gray is not old
everything that glitter is not gold and,
too many lies can destroy the truth
a truth that needs to be told.

This is a very sick society
with a very serious problem
if we keep doing what the dead has done
you're soon to be the next one.

So many of us are waiting to fly
we got so many reasons to try
we got too many ways to die and
I think we all know why.

This is a very sick society
with a mental serious problem and
if we keep doing what the dead has done
then we're soon to be the next one.

ONE GENERATION
10/94

I'll play my mind one time and
you adjust your mind to mine,
we got hope so find with faith and time
that takes us where we need to be.

We already lost one generation
all but one has gone down the drain so
if we lost all but one generation,
then we just lost one too many.

All but one fill our streets and stained
with so many mother's pain and
I hope no one treats your child the same because,
we got just as many coming as we got going.

We already lost one generation
all but one gone down the drain and if,
we lost all but one generation, I think
We just lost one too many.

VIETNAM
6/019

Our growing days are dead and gone
but the memories still linger on
the limit is the sky no one wants to die
I can still hear every soldier's cry.

Remember us we were young
remember us we did not fear
we have tried, we have died, we were here.

Fathers are pleading
mothers are praying
lovers are all alone please
remember our pain remember our name
and how we faced our death in vain.

Remember us we were young
remember us we were here
don't forget us we had no fear
we have tried, we have died, we were here.

PASS IT ON
6/013

We got to learn how to elevate each other
stop the hate toward each other
we got a long way to go, a short time to get there and
just as sure as my name shine
it's all about what's in your mind.

You got to pass it on
you got to pass it on
hate is strong before world is gone
you got to pass it on.

We all know how much hate can bring you down
we all know how long it's been around
if you just let love become your light
We can all do what's right and put an end to this fight.

You got to pass it on
you got to pass it on
hate is strong before the love is all gone,
you got to pass it on.

LAND OF THE WEAK
2/017

Let's get out and do what we should
let's get out and do some good
we have the opportunity to make
a better society starting with our neighborhood.

The poor and the upset
are down in the creek
where it's hard to be strong in the
land of the weak.

When we fight amongst ourselves
we so quickly fall apart and
when we fall apart we break God's heart when
He gives us the opportunity to make a new start.

The poor and the upset
are down in the creek
where it's hard to be strong in the
land of the weak.

HEAL THE LAND
8/04

Love is why I pray each and everyday
love is not for pay or a daily game to play
like a spirit that never goes down,
God's love must always be around.

Every mind must be on me
every heart must be free
only then will I reveal my plan,
only, then will I heal the land.

There must be peace in every sky
there must be love in every eye
every woman and every man,
reaching for each other's hand.

Every heart must be free
every mind must be on me
only then you will understand
Only then will I reveal the plan and I will heal the land.

KEEP IT REAL
1/022

When we march there's no rest we get out we protest
we don't have time for ghetto games
to call each other out of our names,
That's so wrong even a blind man can see.

Our time is important
our minds are important
Our lives are important, we have to keep it real.

Life always changes but the hate never ends
don't let the system dum you down
that will stop you from getting around
leaving you 6 feet underground, we have to be
that strong link from ancestor to ancestor
We got placed under arrest, we got out we protest.

Our time is important
our minds are important
our lives are important, we got to keep it real.

EVIL COMPANY
1/022

Youngsters who turn into gangsters
gangsters who turn into monsters
they can take graceland turn it into wasteland so,
you better stay in your place man.

It's an ugly way of life
it's an unsafe place to be and
I can't be with anyone I see in evil company.

It can make you the lowest of the already low
so that you cannot maintain
so that your life won't remain
so that you will not know
so that your mind can never grow, evil company.

It's a very ugly way to be
it a very unsafe place for me and
I can't be with anyone I see, in evil company.

MERCY AND GRACE
6/021

Every ghetto carries low education so
to save this nation to clean up this place
it's gonna take God's mercy and grace.

We are not all from the same ghetto
we all don't play the same role
we, are not from the same household.

Every ghetto has its own shame
each of us carry some kind of pain and
though we are not from the mid east
we are still being murdered by the beast,
the ones who call themselves police.

Every ghetto carries low education
each one across this nation
to solve this case and care for the human race
it's gonna take God's mercy and grace.

BLOOD SWEAT AND TEARS
6/020

I was just sitting around
reminiscing on all my days and cares
and all praise is due to God
I have reached my older years and.

How did I get here
through their sweat through their fears
through their blood sweat and tears.

Someone said we are living in a trend
the kind that seems to never end
and it seems the hate will never end
Why can't we stop the killing and how did we get here?

Through the spirit of our ancestors
through their sweat
through their cares
through their blood sweat and tears
for so many years.

THE GREATEST NATION
1/022

How can the greatest nation on earth
be so full of blues and bad news
they are great for lien they are great for murder
they are great for graves, over 4 hundred slaves.

You can not win if your not right within
for what you get is what you do and
whatever you do comes back to you
you feed on pain you have no shame
you must have water on the brain.

They are great for lien
they are great for Lyching
they are great for murder
great for the graves and 4 hundred years of slaves and
that's how the greatest nation on earth
can be so full of bad news.

FRUITS OF EVIL
8/01

Let's not save our evil ways
let's not give all evil praise
let us pray against all evil
in these last and evil days.

We are up against all evil
throughout all our people
release my people from the fruits of evil
in these last and evil days.

Throughout everyday
throughout every night
if you know this is right show your light
clean up your ways these days.

We are up against evil
throughout all of our people
release my people from the fruits of evil
in these last and evil days.

HEIFERS AND HEATHENS
10/019

To all heifers to all heathens
to all hoodlums of the slum
your time has come, get rid of the gun
teach your brain to sustain,
you have a future to maintain.

There is no other season
so find a better reason
don't be a heifer, don't be a heathen.

We do have you in mind
we know you want to shine but
you have to leave all that's negative behind,
we have come a long way it's been a long day
no one has to stay that way.

To all heifers to all heathens
there is no better time or season so
let's find a better reason, don't be a heifer
don't be a heathen.

WE ARE THE WORLD
3/010

Here is a word to the world
this is a word for us all
what is your music playing, what is the music saying
we got to wake up in these hard times
we got to wake up so many young minds.

We are the world in the words of you and me
we are the world is the way we should be,
when we stand for unity.

Living in this world can feel like a ghost
when the ones you love hurts you the most
so many are blind to the ways of mankind and,
showing the same old signs,
we got to wake up the mighty young minds.

We are the world are the words of you and me
we are the world is the way all should be,
We are the world when we stand for unity.

THIS NATION'S FAITH (PT2)
1/022

A nation that needs to rise up
a nation that needs a true meaning
a nation that has yet to live out its creed.

This nation's faith
this nation depends upon mercy
this nation depends upon grace
This nation depends upon her faith.

We don't know all the good that surrounds us
we don't know all the madness
we don't know all the sad
so the good have to suffer with the bad and
they don't want any reflection of God in this nation.

This nation depends upon faith
this nation depends on her mercy
a nation that survives by only God's grace
We are this nation's faith.

WORLD PEACE
5/020

We are living in a nation
where pigs never throw up
some kids never grow up we are living in a nation
where wages barely go up.

We don't need another angry beast
we don't need another side piece
What we need is world peace.

When we lose our temper
we get right into a fight all because
somebody said something somebody didn't like
love don't kill it gives us a will, and it looks like
only the wise will survive.

We don't need another side seat
we don't need another side street
we don't need another side piece,
What we need is world peace.

EVERY SOUL
12/05

Every soul means something to Jesus
everyone means something to him
everyone needs their life in Jesus,
Every soul means something to him.

When every evil schemes and steal your dreams
your life means nothing to them
everyone is given a dream to bear
my life without Jesus I would not even dare,
Jesus is my boss he is the driving
When my soul was lost he died on calvary cross.

Every soul means something to Jesus
every life means something to him
every soul needs a life in Jesus
We all mean the world to him.

THANKING JESUS
10/05

I'm thanking Jesus for one more day
thanking Jesus that's the way I pray
for all my health for all my strength
for the clothes I wear for the food I eat,
for the new shoes on my feet.

I'm thanking Jesus
for this breath that I breathe
for being this awesome help that I need
for my father for my mother
for my sister and for my brother.

I'm thanking Jesus
for being closed in my right mind
for keeping me away from crime
for giving me this day and time
for giving me a mind so clear for giving all his
love and care, thank you Jesus.

WHEN YOU PRAY
10/82

Use God's will
to brighten up your day when you pray
use God's will and use it his way,
when I feel like there is no way
he, give me the will to pray.

Since we know everyday
since we know what to say
let his will light your way when you pray,
you have the will God has the way, if
every will has its day, then everyday let us pray.

Since you know what to say
and you know how to pray
when you pray let him have his way
and his will will brighten up your day.

MODERN DAY EVIL
8/84

And the evil starts spreading around
from the underground it's holding you down
it's pushing you around
evil got you losing your ground.

Modern day evil in modern day times
modern day evil in modern day minds.

Somehow in the mind of evil
so many are without a mentor
so many are without guidance
evil got them berried down pin down to the ground,
tearing at the heart tearing them apart.

Modern day evil in
modern day times
Modern day evil stuck in modern day minds.

WE KEEP TRYING
2/90

We keep trying I aint lyn and
if I am lyn I'm flynn and
I aint, flapped a wing yet.

We got to help our brother
so help me father
we got to help each other so help me mother
keep your head up high like the ocean meets the sky,
we keep trying we keep trucking
foul words and bullets we keep ducking.

We keep trying and I aint lyn and
if I'm lyin I'm flynn if all upset
you can bet and I aint flapped a wing yet
like a lion made of ion we keep trying.

FROM GOD'S GRACE
9/85

You had to see it to reveal it
you had to be there to believe it
from the water to the wire,
out of the pan into the fire.

God's grace lost its place
now there's a frown on everyone's face
he got fed up shedding the grace.

Children don't have a role model
we keep living in the bottle
slapping who we wanna slap
grabbing who we wanna grap
until one day God got fed up, you had to be there to see it.

You had to be there to believe it
God's grace lost its place
now there's a frown on every face
somehow he's fed up shedding his grace.

THE ALMIGHTY LOVE
10/83

I'm speaking of the Lord almighty
I'm singing of his glory
I'm speaking of his love I'm talking about
the almighty love of God.

The same God who made the waters
the one who com the sea
the same God who walk the waters
the one who died for you and me.

Are you speaking of the love of Jesus
are you singing about the same love and story
who is the almighty God
I'm singing of his glory
the almighty love of God.

A SUNDAY SONG
6/84

We cannot sing of the power
without telling every story
as you give us the power
we will bring you the glory.

There is a time we come together
to temples we belong
bring us your monday story
singing to us your sunday song.

Trials and tribulations don't live here anymore
love and understanding
is what we come here for
we sing it from the west we sing it from the east
We sing it to a world where we need love and peace.

This is the time to come together
at temples we belong
we cannot feel the power without our sunday song
we come to spread the glory it's in our sunday song.

COME DOWN JESUS
6/89

We got mothers without fathers
we got brothers without friends
we even got crack pushing us back
because of your wisdom that we lack.

Come down Jesus come down
we are about to lose our ground,
teach us to spread your love around.

We found no pie in the sky just an eye for an eye
that's how low we are now
that's how deep they dum us down
but when Jesus comes around
stand your ground can't hold us down.

Come down Jesus come down
we need your love right now
come down Jesus come down
teach us how to spread your love around.

MIGHTY MIND
1/022

You hold that sign
I hold that sign together
We hold the sign, let it shine.

I am that shine I am that kind
I am that sign of a mighty mind.

We are running the streets
getting shot down at the lease
getting lock down by police
everybody cannot play in darkness
someone has to see the light
everybody cannot feed them darkness
someone has to shine the light.

I am that shine I am that kind
I am that good and I'm that sign
of a mighty mind.

RIGHTEOUS RAIN
6/05

Dear Lord I have heard about you
and how you turn old things new
and how you turn gray skies blue and
I have nothing else to do
but to sit here and talk with you.

We need your rain
our sins are in saine
we need your righteous rain today
to cleanse our sins away.

It seems that no one wants the blame
everyones fighting for the fame
when we should be calling on your name
because we need your righteous rain and
we need to seek your holy name.

Our sins are in sain we need your rain
Lord we need your righteous rain
we need your righteous rain today
come and cleanse our sins away.

FEELING HISTORY
11/82

History those who believed in me
black history those who died for me and
It fills another chapter as I face another future.

History in my heart
black history here in my heart
Why do I keep feeling history in my heart?

Don't punish me with brutally
sit and talk with me so that we can see
that great garment of destiny
those who bled died and paved the way
That is why I'm standing here today.

History in my heart
black history down in my heart like
a garment of destiny here in my heart
Why do I keep feeling history in my heart?

THE FINGER OF LOVE
8/82

When the hand of love touches the heart of hate
it becomes a heart of love
when the heart of love touches the finger of hate
it becomes the finger of love.

So who can hate you who can hate christ
the only one who gives us life
who can hate you who can hate christ
the only one to lay down his own life
the son who set us free who died for you as well as me.

When his hand of love touches the heart of evil
it becomes the heart of love
when his heart of love touches
the finger of hate it becomes
the finger of love.

ON GOD'S LAND (PT2)
11/86

On God's land
on God's land
each, and every future is on God's land.

In God's hand
in God's hand
this is where we stand on his land
Every woman, every man is in God's hand.

On God's land
on God's land
the master plan it's in God's hand
and he's not going to trust, just
any woman or man on this land.

LET US PRAY
1/05

So I say these things happen everyday
we need to pray pray
so the world won't go astray
because we are well on our way.

We can't see eye to eye that's no lie
no one wants to die to see the by and by
now we all are in the need
of that mighty mustard seed let us pray.

So I say these things happen everyday
we are on our merry way
these things happen so I say let us pray
pray that the world don't go astray
Because we are so well on our way.

LAST AND EVIL DAYS
11/04

We can hope we can pray
we have to keep the faith everyday
trouble won't last always
in these last and evil days.

Yes there is a God and he understands
search within your heart because
he knows somewhere life is torn apart
so let's hope and pray represent our praise
these last and evil days
yes there is a God and his love is true and
he gives us life his spirit offers you

We can hope we can pray
we can keep the faith each day
so I give him the praise
trouble won't last, always these evil days.

LORD JESUS SHINE
8/04

When it comes to being that good man
we hold the key in the palm of our hand
the steps of a good man are ordered by the Lord
the true bread of life.

Lord Jesus shine
on this poverty line
take control of this so of mine
you know our hearts and you know our minds.

Many words come to mind
in this day and time
all because we can make our lives better
from time to time we seek to find when
your life is all about what's in your mind.

Lord Jesus shine on this poverty line
your love is divine you got that super natural kind
I only heard the story you know the mind
you know our hearts and minds.

FEEBIE
5/07

Don't school me with your disguise
don't fool me with your lies
I am human I have meaning
man or woman I'm a human being.

So feebie said free me
I won't wait until you feed me
so feebie said free me
It's time we all be free.

Don't dum me with your fantasy
I refuse to be the way you see
for I have rage that fills inside and
if I resist you will feel my pride and
if I learn more than you say I should
That's because I strive more than you ever could.

So 'feebie said free me
I'm not gonna wait until you feed me
so feebie said free me it's about time
we all be free.

REAL LOVE
1/08

Love in the rain love can be fun
love can bring pain more ways than one
by someone's daughter
by someone's son.

So much phonie love is going around
the real thing cannot be found
too much phonie love is going around and
real love is nowhere around.

Rain can be pain more ways than one
love can be said love can be done
love can be lost and love can be won
but only real love can be fun.

Too much phonie love going up and down
real love is nowhere around
too much phonie love is going around and
real love needs to be found.

MY HOME TOWN
1/08

I'm gonna shine in my mind because
I want everything to be find
everybody in this town wears a frown
Everybody wants to put their foot down.

In my home town I felt down
by the people who pushed me around
in my home town I felt low down
by so-called friends who put me down.

Until one day I heard an oldman say
keep your spirit up hold tight to your faith
and stand your ground and
until one day I heard an old lady say
trouble doesn't last always.

In my home town I felt low down
by so call friends who pushed me around
in my home town I wore a frown
because I couldn't stand my ground.

SOMETHING FOR THE HEAD
6/05

Something for the head that ale's you
something for the head
to make you feel new
something for the head that can kill you.

A blunt in one hand a shot in the other
you left your brain is in the rain
now you need an umbrella and
all it takes is one puff if you cop the right stuff
but you think it's not enough
Now, here comes the hand cuffs.

Something for the head that to make you fly
something for the head that can unable you
something for the head for whatever ale's you
something for the head to make you feel new
something for the head to kill you dead.

THE BAD PART PAST
5/90

A no good past won't let you last
quickly pass the laughing gas
a no good past won't let you laugh
when visions show a stormy path.

That bad part of the past
is moving real fast
keep on looking in the mirror glass.

All scars will heal is the right way to feel
whenever you feel your shoulders to the wheel
there is no time for laughs study your path
release the storm release your past and
love what you see in the mirror glass.

The bad part past is moving fast and
visions show a stormy path
the bad part past is moving real fast
keep on looking in that mirror glass.

A LIFE LONG LESSON
2/02

There is no experience
like this one at hand if self experience
can't teach you then nothing else can.

We all show our learning and
it don't look so good
when we refuse to do good
in our neighborhoods.

Seek and you will find
how to stay away from crime and
to win this fight and gain your right
we must live by faith and not by sight.

There is no experience
like this one at hand and if
self experience cannot teach you
then nobody can.

GOODWILL
7/02

Goodwill is alright
good will is strong with
goodwill we will survive the storm.

It is good to be good
being good is never wrong
it's so good to be willing to help those unable
to cook a pot of warm soup for an old kitchen table
good is their will and that will is care
with good will and care we can all get somewhere.

Good deeds are alright
good needs no wrong and
goodwill is strong and with
good will we all will survive this storm.

THE PEACEMAKER
10/04

If it's peace that's find
it's the peace that shine
that peace within your mind
don't get scared and run off, I say this all the time.

The peace assigned to richard shine
was made to meet his maker
the peace designed by richard shine
is to be the peacemaker.

One good sign one good time
brings out the light you see
a heart in flight with truth so bright
it brings out the light in me.

Don't get scared and run off
I say this all the time
this peace assign to richard shine
was made to meet mankind
this peace is assign to richard shine
is to be a world peacemaker.

I'M ON MY WAY
1/04

It's a brand new day
the skies are gray
the end is near and I'm on my way.

I seperate my right from my wrong
by all means and all casualties
it's what's best for me in the care of others
after all we suppose to be brothers
a fear of the end is coming near
could I have been more careful
could I have been more aware.

I'm living so hard there's no time to play
i'm living so hard I forgot the day
I been living so hard my hair is gray
the end is near and I'm on my way.

WHEEL WITHIN A WHEEL
10/03

I write about reality
I write about what's real
I write within reality
like a wheel within a wheel.

Like the witches tale came to avail and I never seen the jail
or those who never restrain from evil
when the mind isn't strong it cannot see light
evil becomes our level death becomes our sight
when the mind seeks wrong because of right
it's gonna need super light
from the good to the evil for the sake of all people.

I write within reality
I write about what's real
I write within reality
I write within the wheel for the sake of all society
there's a wheel within a wheel.

IN AMERICA
5/05

Together we gather no matter how far
no matter how deep the scar
In America, this is who we are.

You can sail the seas
you can enjoy the breeze
blowing through the trees
you can reach that star no matter how far
nations make you big and bold
pushing something in your soul
challenging you to reach that goal.

No matter how deep the scar
you are that superstar
you can drive that fancy car because
in America it's just who we are.

MOTHER AND FATHER'S LOVE
6/05

These chances that I take
were all here before I was born
so the chances we all take
is what keeps us moving on.

I think I'll follow my father and
if I follow his love doesn't mean
I don't love my mother, I still have her love.

It was a sad day when father passed away
it was such a bad day
me and mother got together everyday we would pray
then came that day when mother went away
Now, every day I pray on mother and fathers day.

I think I'll follow my mother and
if I follow her love
it doesn't mean I don't love my father because
I still have his love, mother and father's love.

BEVERLY DEPASS
9/05

Thinking of the future
through an hourglass
we can build our future
by learning from the past.

Bring it to the future
singing of the past BBeverly the future
Beverly Depass.

Take me to your future
sweet memories to last
the queen of my future
life will be a blast.

Thinking of the future from a distance past
bringing in the future through an hourglass
we can build our future by learning from the past
BBeverly is the future sweet BBeverly depass.

BLACK CHILD
8/05

Black child pretty little child
your not like the child that's wild
black child pretty little child
you deserve the sunshine in your heart.

Because you need strength
your life will have length
these words are all meant for you
swing around the rich and you will be richer
hang around the poor and
you will always need more.

Black child pretty little child
your not like that child thats wild
black child greatful little child
you deserve the sunshine in your heart.

IN THE DARK
2/022

Another book in the dark
another book that's right
another book in the dark
has got to come to the light.

A new year is here you say you don't care
another year you walk the streets in fear
you're tired of living in the slums
you're tired of living amongst the bums
you're tired of hanging around the bends
being deceived by so call friends and
you have got to be wise in order to realize
how important your mind is how important your time is
so I'll write this book in the dark.

Another book in the dark
another book that's so bright because
whatever you do in the dark
has got to come to the light.

YOU SAY AND I SAY
5/020

I say he is soon to come back
you say that's just a mystery fact
you say that's wrong I say that's right and
if he is gone in your eye sight
Why can't he come back to mine?

I say he is Jesus Christ
you say that's nice
I say that he is great
you say that's a little late.

I say that he is black
you say I am wrong and
I say that I am right
but you say that he is white "well"
if he is white in your eye sight,
why can't he be black in mine.

THE FREEDOM
5//020

We got freedom to fly
we got freedom to try
we got freedom to live
we got freedom to die.

We got the freedom to think
we got the freedom to drink
We got the freedom to turn over the whole pot sink.

We got freedom to try
we got freedom to cry
we got freedom to give
we got freedom to lie and
we are free to be the key and
put an end to any mystery.

We got the freedom to wink
we got the freedom to think and
we are free to use this key and
put an end to our misery.

ANYBODY CARE
6/020

Sign in and find out what the fuss is all about
sign up and find out
what this world is all about.

Can somebody hear us
can anybody see us
Can somebody save us, does anybody care?

There is a future out here awaiting
there are lives out here fading
they are still down grading us
they are still dumping us down plus
the police are being unfair
That's what keeps them in the clear.

Can somebody help us
can anybody hear can anybody see us
Can somebody save us? Does anybody care?

FORGIVENESS
6/020

When living in the slum
people can be so dum if God can
forgive us who we trustpass why can't we
forgive those who trustpass against us.

We all need it at some point and time
we all want it at some point and time
Everybody needs forgiveness.

Never blame a man
for doing what he can like
forgiving and giving someone else a hand
how long must we stand
with our heads stuck in the sand.

We all need it at some point and time
we all ask for it at some point and time
we all can use it everybody needs some
forgiveness.

STAND UP AND UNITE
10/020

We all know how dangerous it is
to be a blackman in this society
no matter how you clear the air
you can still hear I don't care.

We must stand up and unite
show our learning show our light come together
everyday and night stand up and unite.

We are dyn fast everyday going down in every way
we were given the kind of mind
that produces jail time with
no meaning to forgive no regards to live, and
they know this yet still, you can hear, I don't care.

We have to stand up and unite
stop the killing end the fight
show our learning day and night
stand up right come together and unite.

IN JESUS NAME
2/015

In Jesus name for the rest of our lives
until the end of this journey
we won't play no game, we all feel the same.

These and other blessings we share the pain
these and other blessing we show no shame
these and other blessings in Jesus name.

You gave me the sign it cleared my mind
you are the creator of all our times
you hold my time you gave the sign
to help us renew our souls and minds.
we share the blame release the chain
from our brain give us back our holy name.

These and other blessings we share the pain
these and other blessings
we won't show no shame
these and other blessings in Jesus name
in the name of Jesus in Jesus name.

THE DREAM
2/015

Patch it up paint it brown
don't let the dream drown
Gene green was a marine a fighting machine
the young age of 18 a young man with a dream.

Put down the dope and pick up the dream
put down the guns and pick up the dream
don't let the dream drown.

Short is a though when your thoughts are plain
because your head is in pain and
your dreams can go down the drain but
say no not today don't let it rain
patch it up, paint it brown, don't let it go down.

Put down the dope and pickup the dream
put down the gun and pickup the dream
put down the frown and pickup the dream
patch it up paint it brown
don't let the dream drown.

TWO HOURS OLD
3/015

We got high tech throbbing
we got pins on top of needles
we got sixty years young and
We are fifty years old.

It don't matter how young
it don't matter how old
no matter how many slips away
the young pushes the old out of the way.

They are not gonna give it if it's the
right thing to do or just because it's fair
that's the time they need you here
because in the middle of nowhere
this warfare can turn servere. and

So I been told it don't matter how old
it don't matter how many slip away
time after time day after day
the young pushes the old out of the way.

FORGIVING
3/015

When your storm comes around and
your life is falling down
when you cannot see an end and
lonely clouds are coming in.

If you just keep on forgiving
you can overcome this life
if you try and you apply your spirit will fly.

Do you need a hand to hold
everyone at some point needs a hand
everybody here on God's land so
when those clouds come around and
your world turns upside down.

If you just keep forgiving
you can overcome this life
if you try and you apply your spirit will fly
and your spirit will never die
just like that spirit from on high will never die.

THE BEST YOU CAN
12/014

When it comes to money life can be funny
some days are cloudy some days are sunny
Life has a game to my name that has no shame.

Life can be a top of the hill thrill
life can be a downhill kill and
you gotta play your hand the best you can.

One day it's rainy the next day it's sunny
and you'll never know if you don't go
and you'll never shine if you don't glow so
when you get that glow you got to know
which way to go.

Life to me can be a downhill kill
life to me can be a top of the hill thrill
in order to understand how to be a better man
you gotta play your hand
do the best you can.

TRUST NO MAN
4/020

We are living in a mind
that's too blind to see
we are living in the way of false reality
The real stories were gold but many lies were told.
This is my struggle on this land
where we live and where we stand
is where no man can trust no man.

Many men can do evil and
women can do evil too
too many of us lose we get bumped and bruised
that's how we created the blues
many people claim don't always view the same and
we even made a game in God's name and
too many lives are affected by lies.

This is my struggle on this land
I got to do the best I can
here where I live is where I stand
where no man can trust no man.

FREE IN MISERY
4/020

What is slavery when we were in misery
what is misery when we were in slavery "well"
If we claim to be free, why are we still in misery?

This shouldn't have to be
it don't feel right to me no one free
should be in misery.

We are the pain we are the blame
we left our brain out in the rain
weak lines come from weak minds
deep lines come from deep minds
take me to another place
Some of us are just, a hopeless case.

This should not have to be
it don't seem right to me free in misery
no one free should be in misery.

MINE SHINE
6/019

If you want to survive
you have got to get wise
we are living on concrete
where there's a jungle in the street.

Mine shine it's your time
let your mind shine sunny
find good ways to make good money.

Everybody do your thang
every city has a ghetto
every gun got a bang every ghetto got a gang
if you want to survive you have
got to get wise it's no surprise.

Mine shine it's your time
let your mind shine sunny
find good ways to make good money.

LIBBY'S LOBBY
1/021

Living in Libby's lobby
Libby got a lobby and
it looks mighty sloppy
clean up your sloppy lobby Libby's lobby.

Living in Libby's lobby
Sloppy Libby
sloppy lobby and I'm swimming
in Libby's lobby, that's where Bobby got his hobby.

And when living in Libby's lobby
every lobby needs you Libby
like every libby needs a jalopy
clean up your slobby jalopy Libby's
living in Libby's lobby.

THE MOUNTAIN SIDE
4/015

On the mountain side you were the one
you were the best friend I ever had
even when I had to breathe in a paper bag.

I cried where my father died
on the mountain side and I cried
when my mother died on the other side.

My life came crashing down
it seem like no love could be found
many spirits came around
to pound me in the ground then you came around
to fill that hole that held me down.

I cried where my father died
on the mountain side
that's where I cried and I cried
where my mother died on the other side.

EIGHT DAYS AFTER
4/015

Tears can always bring us together
when fears always tears us apart then
eight days after we forgot about the laughter.

Eight days after becomes
eight more tears a day
eight days 'after are more fears to pay.

So many loopholes are in the law
can make you wonder
how did we ever get this far
when the sound of of in vain
beats against your window pane and
killing every child to your name.

Eight days after became eight more tears a day
eight days after became eight more fears to pay and
After eight hours we had to wait eight more years.

I'M GONNA MAKE IT
4/015

Pardon my heart pardon my stare
I found out what is really going on
it got next to my care and i'm gonna
Need a real good friend because.

If i'm gonna make it
it's got to be a new world for me
a better place to see and a better place to be.

Some of us just want a better beer to drink
some of us just want a better blunt to smoke and
so many here amongst us think that life is just a joke
so take a flashlight to this life and
pardon my heart because.

If i'm gonna make it
it's got to be a new world for me
a better place to be and if i'm gonna make it
it's got to be a better world for see and
no more misery if i'm gonna make it.

ON THIS EARTH
5/015

You have to watchout for trickery
so many minds are slippery on this earth
people are losing their mind on an internet line
What are we doing to stop this?

No matter how unfair
no matter how much you care
we are born on this earth none of us can leave here.

I won't let nobody take you down
I won't let no one mess you around and
don't you let nobody steal your crown my brother
we are all the same we all bear the bad name
we all don't play the same bad game. so

No matter how unfair
none of us can leave here
no matter how much you care
no matter how much you hear
we are born on this earth none of us can leave here.

WALK IN THE LIGHT
5/015

We have the greatest seeds
we solved the greatest needs
We have the greatest lead remember the fight.

Walk in the light
talk in the light there is no need to fight
when you walk in the light.

Remember that night there was a terrible fight
they turn a starry night into a sorrowful sight
but we can turn this starry night into a beautiful sight
we solve their greatest needs we are the greatest seeds,
All we need to do is just.

Walk in the light
talk in the light
feel what is right morning noon and night
there is no need to fuss or fight
when you walk in the light.

COMPASSION
5/015

Stand back listen
in a world of sex and drugs I got a story and
it needs be told like the
healing of a sin sick soul.

When there is trouble everywhere
compasion opens up your eyes to feel as I feel
I will feel compassion and God will open up with care
to help you feel it in your ear compassion.

When we bear this life with sorrow
we beg we steal we barrow like there is no tomorrow
just give yourself some time
then feed your soul the sign to find what on your mind
compassion just like prayer will be there.

When there's trouble everywhere
compasion opens up your eyes to see as I see
and when I see you standing there I will open up
with care to help us feel compassion everywhere.

WHY WE CRY
4/020

Are we free or is it just me
no one free to me should be
living in so much poverty we were freed
with no land into the hands of the Klu Klux Klan.

That's why we cry
some of us die for the pie
some of us are barely getting by.

We were free or is it just me
no roof over your head no way of protection
no pot to pee in no bed to push underneath and
still we stand woman and man
on the same land of the Klu Klux Klan.

That's why we cry now
some of us will die getting high
some of us will die for the pie
some of us will reach for the sky and
some of us are barely getting by.

WHEN I SHINE
5/020

When I shine I'm on line and
just as sure as my name shine
one mind assign to the peace of mind
Hoppen to open up your mind.

When I shine i'm on line
you can look me up sometime
just as sure as my name shine
When you read my book you read my mind.

And to open up your mind
you can look me up sometime because
when I shine i'm on line
to give you some knowledge of mine
so that when you read my book
you can read my mind.

FATHER FROM ABOVE
3/016

I am your father from above
you are the child that I love
yesterday I saw your eyes full of tears
because of your troubles throughout the years
and yes I know you are in pain
you don't have to explain.

I lifted you out of the game
I pulled you out of the rain
even though I know you will go back again.

You are my child from above
you are the child that I love
I give to you my whole heart
just in case yours fall apart
I poured my grace over you in your sins.

I carried you out of the rain
I lifted you out of your pain
I pulled you out of your sins even though I know
you will go back again and again and again.

WITH THIS SONG
5/016

Our love our hate our good our great
the rain and the shower
the bride and her flower, our Lord and his power.

Is there something wrong with this song
with this song we can last long
With this song we can be strong.

You are the best you held me tight
I am truly bless you held on to me
when I was going through my mess
you forgave me when I trust pass
and I was moving too fast
a little girl and her flower mighty Lord and his power.

Is there anything wrong with this song
is there anything wrong because with this song
we can be strong we can't go wrong
We can get up, we can move on with this song.

THE GOOD LIFE
4/015

Close the door step on the floor
we don't need anymore war
it's high time to feel find
It's high time to feel free.

Good life we want the good life
no more stress at night no more fights.

We want a life we can sustain
not one that goes right down the drain
we want movie stars women and cars
it's high time to be cool high time to be free
I want the whole world to see
I want a good life, for me.

Good life I want the good life
no more fears at night
no more stress no more fights
it's high time to feel find don't leave us behind
We want the good life.

MODERN DAY GROOVE
5/015

I'm in a Marvin Gaye mood
I got a modern day groove
I got a modern day move
with a Marvin Gaye groove.

I know good and well we know it's hell
when the air makes you choke
when police don't know you trust become a joke
but they can't stop me and I'll tell you why
though my feet are on the ground
my mind is in the sky.

I got a modern day groove
I'm in a modern day mood
I got a modern day move
with a modern day Marvin Gaye groove.

I GOT A DREAM
5/015

I'm not gonna die because
I got a dream and
I'm not ready to die because i'm too fly
and before I do I'll walk on by.

I got a dream that I long to see
everyday can be peaches
Everything can be cream.

In this world of drugs and money
everybody wants more milk
everybody wants more honey and
if you want to be treated right
you gotta treat yourself right
no one can do you better than you.

I got a dream that I long to see
I got a something that I want to be
where everyday can be peaches
Everything can be cream. I got a dream.

A STRONG SONG
3/016

We remembered the past
we said it wouldn't last
we look forward to the future
from the hour glass
so much crime in the nation since
we need more information
Here is a song for every situation.

To stop what is going around
to stop what is going wrong
It's gonna take, a strong song.

It's not good to feel so bad though
it's not bad to feel so good
in these last days trouble don't last always
and the message here is clear
This could be your good year. so
To stop what is going around and
to stop what is going wrong
It's gonna take a strong song to stop what's going on.

EYE TO EYE
3/016

For any given reason
only God can change the season
for any given reason he makes the sun rise
one powerful force no man can wrecken.

When we see eye to eye
then we rise side by side
the more we see eye to eye we turn the tide.

God is the father that we praise
he is the length of all our days and
very righteous in all his ways
greater than any sin we can live in
greater than any pain we have to bear.

When we see eye to eye
then we rise side by side
when we see eye to eye our power
will rise and turn the tide side by side.

MIND BLIND
3/016

You have to treat your neighbor right
everyday and every night
live and learn to love each other
as I have loved you this is your truth
this is your light this is what it takes
to keep down the fight. Dear God

I come to you from this mind because
everything down here is not so find
we live in a closed mind time after time
Good Lord of mercy, we are mind blind.
Everybody wants to be somebody
everybody wants to be up there and
the other half just don't care
our hearts can't feel 247 and
Everybody wants to build their own heaven. so
I come to you from this mind
everything down here is not so find
we can't feel any peace of mind good Lord of mercy
our mind is blind.

GOD AND I
3/016

There is good there is bad and
there is sad in all nations
tears don't dry on the phone
tears don't dry on their own and if
they don't dry when you're alone.

Smile God loves you keep on smiling
God loves you God and I love you.

Every now and then
my hair gets nappy
my friends turn crappy
last night I lost my pappy don't cry
you won't die, God loves you so do I.

Smile God love you
God and I love you
keep on smiling God loves you
God and I love you.

DENIAL RIVER
10/019

Just another great lie
from days gone by
great for lyn to keep them from dyn
another weep for the strong and
many forces of evil all night long.

There are lives in this river
keeping down lies that make you shiver
America's secrets are in, denial river.

She beat down her queen
she shoots down every king
summer winter fall or spring and
the souls of her young seek for an early grave
as the souls of her females meets the sale of slaves.

There are souls the this river
deep down souls in denial river
with deep down lies to make you shiver
American secrets are in denial river.

THE STRUGGLE
10/010

I hope this real that I feel
is not here to stay
I hope this real that I feel
will someday go away.

I feel the struggle and I know it's real
I feel the struggle and I don't mean oneal.

Every cost is up ain't nobody's down
too many enemies around
even the job force bears a cross
dead end jobs from day to day
I see how money can slip away
catch the right train stay in the right lane
no greatness tomorrow, just more sorrow?

I feel the struggle and the struggle is real
just as real as peter's field
I feel the struggle and I don't mean oneal
I feel the struggle and the struggle is real.

MAN OF YOUR MIND
2/022

Have a heart in your happy home
build a home in your happy heart
God truth is about our history it's no lie
and his truth shall never die.

If you don't like the truth that's find
you go your way and I'll go mine and
you be the man of your mind.

Keep thinking positive
with all your might and by your might
someday you'll see the light
it's time we make room for the best
we have no more time for less.

If you don't want to learn that's find
you go your way I'll go mine
go be the man of your mind
you can't get whiskey from a bottle of wine
you be the man of your mind.

OUR SPIRITS
1/015

Nothing in this world is fair
a world without love
a world without care and
That's what brings about fear.

We need a world where
nights are warm life is true
love, keeps our spirits new.

There is no remorse in this life for this world
there is no remorse in this world for life
nothing in this world is fair
no one around here seems to care.

We need a world where
nights are warm life is to
nights are warm love is true
the spirits in you like the sky is blue
love keeps our spirits new.

FOREVER MEAN
12/014

This earth is my first home
heaven will be my last and
just like a piece of broken glass
someday this too shall pass.

We got caught up in this nightmare
we got caught up in the steam
how could a world that dress so clean
turn out to be so mean.

Truly brutally is no fantasy
truly brutally is rooted in reality
so here is the plan let's make sure every man
receives a better hand than a Klu Klux Klan.

We got caught up in a nightmare
we got caught up in a steam
how could a world dressed so clean
turn out to be forever mean.

THE FUTURE IN YOU
3/015

You were always blue
know one ever knew
there was a darker side of you.

The future looks blue the future in you
every year that's near should by now be clear
who made your future disappear.

We were young we were free
more than a few made history
stealing cars robbing bars spending future behind bars
then when you think you got it right
you end up in some terrible fight.

Now the future looks blue the future in you
and every year that gets near
should by now be all clear you made your future disappear
the future in you you made
your future disappear.

IF GIVEN TIME
6/015

We will show more care
as we become more aware
from better souls to better minds
all these things will be in time.

If given time
when we wake up we will find
a world of no more war
children no more fear, every cancer disappears.

Some of us are getting up
some of us are going wild
some of us are a lazy child
we will show more care as we become aware
of a better atmosphere.

If given time these kind of things we will find
no more war of any kind
children of no more fear as we will show more care
our nation will become fair if given time.

DON'T STOP
4/016

In this first episode of life
we find another episode of living
sometimes it's hard to care
a smile gets hard to bear.

Don't stop trying you're not dyn
don't start crying hope will get you by
keep on trying.

Free us from the fear
of oppressions atmosphere
you have to fight to do what's right
so hold on tight to keep from slipping into the night
God is by your side and you will find
strength as years go by.

Don't stop trying don't start crying
you're not dying keep on trying
it's so hard to care when it gets hard to bear
don't stop trying.

A PSALM OF RICHARD (1)

Our father brought brothers to heaven
as they work and pray both night and day
lead us not into temptation
continue your love within our nation
freedoms kingdom must be done
Giving us brith unto this earth
as we bear the pain to remember the name
of which you were born.

We lie in bed and spread your blood
upon our head to deliver your people from their evil
forty two memories become quite the same people
not quite the right friends all our cross to bear
all our case to care we dare this not to be unfair
to bear our burdens in this atmosphere.

Help us keep souls awake
when we can't see beyond the break
we pray dear Lord our souls to take
never our father within the son our father
in heaven loves everyone.

A PSALM OF RICHARD (2)

Dear Lord when you said peace be still
there was a great com and
you never had to use dot com.

Dear Lord give us that peace
give us that kind of love
we are so much in need of and
we shall never see sore eyes again.

We are one nation under God
but cannot pray in schools
we are one nation under God
in indivisible with liberty and justice
we call but not for all.

Dear Lord give us your peace
with your kind of love
we are so much in need of and
we shall never see sore eyes again.

A PSALM OF RICHARD (3)

Games are for those who play
peace is for those who pray
homes for those who need a place to stay
a brighter day for those who lead the way.

May God be with you on this journey
to keep you free from crime
to keep you awake and on time
to keep love and peace in your mind.

Homes for those with no place to stay
a brighter day for those who know the way
games are for those who love to play
let us keep the peace for those who pray.

I WISH YOU WELL

When out of sight seems out of mind
when peace of mind seems hard to find
I wish they knew the young and old
I wish for you this pot of gold
they do wish too I wish you knew
how much I wish the best for you.

I wish and dwell you go run tell
just how much I wish you well.

For you the most I wish the best
when there's no time for you to rest
when life throws to you the test
I wish you never have to settle for less.

I wish and dwell never give you hell
I'll ring the bell you go run tell
That's how much I wish you well.

THE END

Printed in the United States
by Baker & Taylor Publisher Services